My Life in the Mirror with His Footprints

By

Sallie Jane

For the mountains shall depart, and the hills be removed; but my kindness shall not depart from thee, neither shall the covenant of my peace be removed, saith the Lord that hath mercy on thee. Isaiah 54:10

If we confess our sins, he is faithful and just to forgive us our sins, and to cleanse us from all unrighteousness. 1 John 1:9

My Life in the Mirror with His Footprints

Copyright © 2020 by Sallie Jane
ISBN: 978-1-63073-349-0

Published and printed by:
Faithful Life Publishers
North Fort Myers, FL 33903
888.720.0950

info@FaithfulLifePublishers.com
www.FaithfulLifePublishers.com

Published in the United States of America

24 23 22 21 20   1 2 3 4 5

Dedication

Dedicated to Don and Esther, the owners of the Daycare, who have been my friends for 53 years. They encouraged me to do this book.

PREFACE

When I was young, I was told, "I wouldn't amount to anything." Married young, I was made fun of and misused by my first husband.

I wrote this book to show how my Lord lead me through, HE knew me when I was in my mother's womb. HE was with me even times I felt alone but never lost my faith.

The many times I was on my knees praying to Him.

"HE healeth the broken in heart, and bindeth up their wounds" Psalms 147:3

This book explains how I thank my Lord for putting those experiences in my path which made me see with HIS help.

"Show me thy ways. O Lord; teach me thy path." Psalms 25:4

"If ye know these things, happy are ye if ye do them" John 13:17

"Trust in the Lord with all thine heart; and lean not unto thine own understanding. In all thy ways acknowledge HIM, and HE shall direct thy paths" Proverbs 3:5-6

Chapter One

My life started in northern New York in a small town called Carthage. I was born on December 9, 1941, two days after the attack on Pearl Harbor. Stories from family members tell what a difficult time it was to raise a family then. I was the fourth child, having three siblings—two brothers and one sister.

What things cost in 1941:
Annual salary- $2,050
Minimum Wage- .30 per hour
Postage Stamp- .03
Gasoline- .19 per gal
Average Rent- $ 32.00 per month
A house- $6,900
Milk- .34 per gal
Bread- .08 a loaf

My mother was raised in a Christian home with six sisters, and she, in turn, raised us in church and Sunday school. I was baptized as a baby as my parents made the commitment to raise me in church. I have special memories of singing all the children's songs, Jesus Loves Me, I'm in the Lord's Army, My Cup is Full and Running Over, and many more. The music is different in church today; it is beautiful, but I would love to hear the old time religion once in awhile, such as The Old Rugged Cross, One Day at a Time, or Amazing Grace. I miss so many of those old songs.

In 1957, at the age of sixteen, I was saved and born again, at which time I was baptized by being immersed in water. I made the promise to follow His commandments to the best of my abilities. By being baptized, we receive the gift of the Holy Spirit.

He that believeth and is baptized shall be saved; but he that believeth not shall be damned. Mark 16:16

I do not remember much before age five; I just knew I loved Jesus and all the children's Bible stories.

Our home in Carthage was a duplex and we had neighbors that lived next door. Our house had three bedrooms and one bath upstairs. I remember hearing my parents state the rent was $11.00 a month. We did not have a lot. I remember having oatmeal or Cream of Wheat for breakfast every morning. We never had dry cereals because they were too expensive.

Many nights for dinner, we had pancakes. This was food that would go a long way for a family of six. I remember telling my dad, "When I get married, I will never eat pancakes again."

After school, we each would make a sandwich, which amounted to two pieces of bread with mustard and a sprinkle of sugar or mayonnaise. One day, I went to a friend's home for lunch and her mom gave us chocolate milk. I remember thinking they must be rich. We never had chocolate milk; in fact, we only had powered milk.

I never felt good around other kids, because we never had nice clothes. My mom always kept us clean, but she would wash our clothes each night to have them ready for the next day. Washing clothes back then meant using a tub with rollers at the top to squeeze the water out, and then hanging the clothes up to dry.

One day while walking to school, I had to pass a particular girl that always looked so nice. I did not want to stare at her, so I kept my head down as I passed by. When I got right in front of her, I looked up and she said, "You see something green?"

I started crying and ran into the school. Being insecure and not ever thinking I was good enough to play with other kids, I spent a lot of time alone.

Waking up on Christmas, 1946, Daddy lined us all up at the top of the stairs, before leading us so slowly down the stairs. Daddy said, "Be quiet now. We have to make sure Santa's gone."

When we got to the bottom, he told us to wait while he went into the living room to see if Santa was gone. This was about the only Christmas I can remember. My oldest brother got a Schwinn two-wheel bike; sister got a beautiful doll carriage; younger brother got a red flyer wagon; I got a large red tricycle. I remember Mom made us eat breakfast first; I am sure it was to build our excitement. First, she had us bow our heads as she said grace. It seemed like it took forever as each of us had to eat at least one pancake.

My younger brother and I were always together. So much so that folks thought we were twins. Christmas Day, we took his red flyer wagon up to the top of the nearby hill. It was a place Daddy told us not to go. My brother told me to get in the wagon and hold on as he pushed me down the hill. I could not steer it, so over I go onto the black top road. He told me to not tell Daddy, but my parents saw me with bruises all over my face and swollen lips. They knew what we did, as they watched us coming down the hill pulling the wagon behind us. We got a spanking. Yes, parents did that back then. However, that night I remember Mom coming in to put medicine on my swollen lips.

A couple days later, my brother and I were down the street at Tommy's house. My brother was holding a toy rake with his back to me, and when he swung the rake over his shoulder it hit me in the forehead.

"Ouch!"

He turned around, saying, "Oh, that didn't hurt!" But then he saw the blood running down my face. He took my hand and we ran home. He said, "Don't tell Mommy it was me."

When we got home Mom asked, "What happened?"

I yelled out, "It was Tommy!" I never wanted my siblings to be in trouble.

The next year, 1948, we moved to Watertown, about sixteen miles west, and about thirty-five miles from the Canadian border. We lived in an apartment building called The Flats, located right behind the elementary school. I would climb the fence into the schoolyard and swing back and forth on the swings for hours daydreaming about what I might be one day. Do you remember the song lyrics, *whatever will be, will be, the future's not ours to see, que sera, sera*, by Doris Day?

That was me—just dreaming.

Will I be pretty?

Will I be rich?

Chapter Two

After moving to Watertown, we never saw our Christmas toys again. As we got older, we realized our father was a heavy drinker. There were no credit cards back then, so our parents would buy our Christmas gifts on time. Then, when the time came to pay for them, our father would return them. I always believed my father had a lot of guilt for drinking. But at times, he would take it out on my mother and the rest of us. He always told us, "*WE WOULD NEVER AMOUNT TO ANYTHING.*"

We lived in an apartment on the fifth floor; each floor had a small porch. One day, my older brother and sister wanted to jump into the soft snow from the second floor porch. They came to get me. They wanted me to do it first, of course.

My brother said, "Come on, sis. It's just soft snow."

I went with them up to the second floor, climbed over the rail, and jumped. It was not soft snow. It was as hard as ice, and I hurt my back. (Probably part of my back problems today) They came running down to help me out and, as usual, they say, "Don't tell Mom." I never did tell Mom, when she knew my back was hurting.

When I was nine, I went to the grocery store with my father. I picked up a Baby Ruth candy bar and slipped it into my coat pocket. After paying for our groceries, we started for home, but I kept thinking about, *Thou shall not steal.* Exodus 20:15

That candy bar in my pocket made me feel so guilty and anxious. I knew it was wrong and I worried about it all the way home. After getting home, I told my father, "I will be in for dinner." I ran all the way back to the store to put that Baby Ruth candy bar back.

Several weeks later, I told my mother what I had done, but she stated she already knew. She had prayed about it, hoping I would come and tell her. She said the store owner's wife had seen me take it, and she also saw me bring it back. I told my mother how sorry I was, and that I had prayed about it because I knew it was wrong.

In Watertown, my father worked for a car dealership and my mother worked for a ladies' clothing store. We never had much, and I would hear my parents arguing about money. I always felt bad when my siblings or my parents were upset. I could not wait to hear my dad say my name so softly, so that I could run to him, knowing he was not upset anymore. I was happy when everyone in my family was laughing and happy. Happiness to me meant seeing the ones I cared about happy.

One Christmas play at church, I played the part of an angel, I remember feeling so special and thinking this must be how angels really felt.

Our parents never said they loved us. Of course, years later we knew they did, but it was not said back then.

When I was about eleven, I would faint quite often. One of those times, after waking up to my father putting cold water on my face, I could not walk. This went on for several days. One day, I was with my grandmother, just the two of us. I said to her, "Grandma, why wasn't Mom and Dad worried about me when I couldn't walk?"

She quickly took my hand and sat down, saying, "Listen to me. They were concerned, They did not want you to worry. There were a lot of prayers for you. No one knew what it was."

She told me to bow my head and close my eyes while she prayed, "Heavenly Father, thank You for healing my granddaughter. We believe You are our healer and our redeemer."

I believe in lessons from God. I believe when things happen, God gives us messages one piece at a time. God has great plans for our lives, even if we cannot see it at the time. This message from my grandmother stayed with me. (How my parents worried, but did not want me to worry) You will see how that lesson helped me much later in my life when I had my own daughter.

June, 1953, after twelve years of being the youngest child, my mother gave birth to my baby brother. He was the cutest baby I had ever seen. I loved holding and feeding him. Shortly after that, my oldest brother went into the Air Force. He had always looked out for me. But then he was gone, and we did not see him for a long time. When my baby brother was four and I was sixteen, my father took me out of High School to care for him. That saved them from having to pay a babysitter, and at that age I was glad to be out of school.

We did not have a television until 1954. It was a large piece of furniture with only a twenty-one-inch screen. The GE television had to have rabbit hears to get any reception. Of course, back then when you bought a TV, you did not have to pay anyone, such as DirecTV, to watch it. Of course, you only got a couple of channels though.

We never ever had a phone and to this day, I wonder how we ever got along with out one.

I attended church every Sunday morning, Sunday night, plus Wednesday night prayer meeting. Our church was moving to a newly built church building, and my cousin and I went there to scrape the varnish off the old pews.

Chapter Three

I met my first husband in the winter of 1959. I was eighteen, and he was twenty-three and a college graduate. He owned a beautiful 1956 light green Buick. My cousin and I were at the Victoria Restaurant having a cherry coke and listening to the songs on the small jukebox at the table of our booth. We had put a nickel in and selected the song, *Cathy's Clown* by the Everly Brothers. He came over to say hi to us. We had seen him there several times before.

One night, he asked me on a date, and we dated for about a year before he asked me to marry him. I remember feeling good about it; it meant I could be on my own. He told me he wanted us to move to Florida where his parents were. I remember sitting at my mother's kitchen table and writing down all the things I would have, like a washer and dryer—things my mother never had.

We married on December 31, 1960. I was nineteen years old. He had been working for a major company in Watertown and had been laid off. It was difficult for me because my baby brother was seven at that time and I knew I would miss him. Most nights, I got up in the middle of the night to check on my baby brother to make sure he was covered and warm.

I understood why my husband wanted to move to Florida; I had seen him fall several times on the ice and snow. I was not aware of any problems he had until years later. I remember feeling bad for him and I believe that was what I thought was love. We left Watertown on January 1, 1961, arriving in Florida a couple of days later, meeting his mother, younger sister and brother. His mother lived in a one-bedroom apartment and, even though we were newlyweds, we slept on her couch in the living room.

With my husband being a college graduate, he got a job right away. I got a job at Goody Shoe Store making $.75 per hour. It was a job that did not allow us to sit; we had to look busy all the time. If we were not with a customer, we were to be dusting off the shoe racks.

I wanted a place of our own and started looking every day. He wasn't interested though; he was satisfied living with his mother and drinking with his family members. I was never a drinker and it bothered me terribly.

I cried many nights missing my baby brother. I tried to hide it though, because my husband would make fun of me and hit me. I was not going to church at that time, but I prayed all the time.

Eventually, I found a cute over-garage apartment. It was a small efficiency with a couch that made into a bed at night. I begged him to go with me to look at it. Finally he agreed, but because he was upset with me, he pulled the car ahead a little as I was getting in. I landed on the ground while he sat there laughing.

When we looked at the apartment, I saw how difficult the stairs were for him. I knew then this place would not work. However, he liked it and decided to rent it. I knew at that moment I would be carrying any and all items up the stairs myself. I did not want him to feel bad; I just did it.

Having only one car, he took me to work and picked me up after. Standing on my feet from 9 to 4:30, I was tired at the end of the day and just wanted to go home. However, he always headed to the bar to meet his father, aunt, or others. I hated it.

One night, I told him I wanted to go home. He got very upset and, after I asked a couple more times, he hit me in front of everyone. We left, and when we got home he hit me again, saying I embarrassed him.

This was not the life I wanted. I went in the bathroom and turned on the water so he would not hear me cry. I prayed, "Lord, I'm casting all my anxiety on You because I know You care for me. I love You Jesus and I know my help comes from You."

In January 1962, our landlord had a duplex available and offered it to us, even keeping the rent the same. It was a one bedroom and on one level. This was much easier for him and it was very nice. We had a nice front porch and a great yard. Maintaining the lawn was our responsibility and, with no questions asked, I just took it on. I did not want him to feel bad that he could not do it. I did whatever I knew he could not do. At least that was my intention, but instead of him appreciating me, he belittled me in front of friends and others every chance he got. Many were the times I got down on my knees praying, "GOD, I come to you for the strength to get through this."

Early in 1962, I became pregnant with my son. I was so happy. My OB/GYN went over my medical history, as well as my husband's.

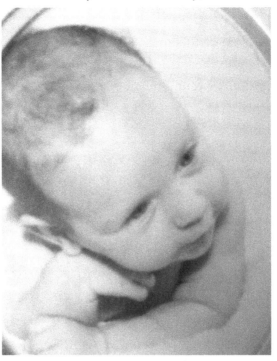

I told him my mother-in-law said that my husband had muscular dystrophy. The doctor then informed me that this particular disease was not inherited. I was very relieved.

My son was born September 7, 1962. He was a beautiful baby boy—eight pounds and seven ounces, blonde hair, and blue eyes. We named our son Robert Scott, but we called him Robby. For the very first time, I experienced a completely different kind of love. It was so sweet, so joyful, and I knew this precious gift from God needed me. I fell in love with my little guy right away. Being out with my little boy, such as in a grocery store, I would actually stop and look around, thinking to myself, no one here can be happier than I am with this precious gift.

Having this little boy, I now wanted a home of our own. I looked for a home to buy, while still budgeting money and saving every penny I could.

A year later, I became pregnant with my daughter. She was born June 16, 1964. Like her brother, she was so beautiful, with blonde hair and blue eyes, weighing eight pounds and six ounces. We named our precious little girl Sandi Jo after a favorite doll I had as a child.

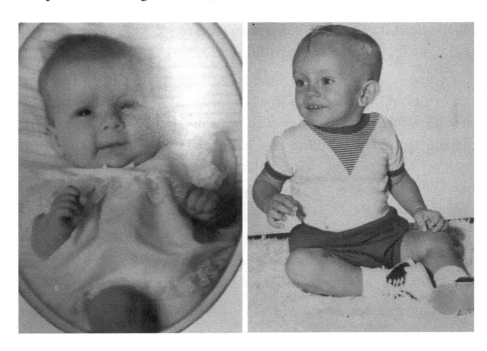

I was so thankful for my two precious babies. Becoming a mother certainly changed my life; everything was now about my babies and me.

When my daughter was one, I found a nice four-year-old home in Sunrise, Florida. It had three bedrooms, two bathrooms, and a pool. It is hard to believe today, but that lovely home cost $21,000 and we had to get a mortgage to afford it. Things were certainly different back in 1965.

My two babies were now my whole life. Living in Florida and having a pool, as well as being near all kinds of water—ocean, canal, or a neighbor's pool—my children needed to learn to swim. I made sure they took swimming lessons. My husband never had patience with the children. One bright and sunny day, he was working on our pool pump, and Robby kept picking up the tools. I was on the deck when I heard him yell, "LEAVE THEM ALONE!" All of a sudden, he hit Robby on the head with a screwdriver. It put a large lump on his forehead. I called Robby's pediatrician to see what to do and was told not to let him go to sleep and place a ice pack on his forehead.

I had enough when it came to hurting the children. That was the beginning of the end for us. I held my son that day, praying that he would be okay. The swelling went down, and he was back playing again as if nothing ever happened. We had planned a trip back to Watertown to visit family. I had several gallbladder attacks, but I could not show the pain I was in because my husband would always laugh at me.

We got to New York and had a great time seeing everyone. I wanted to tell my mother about my pain, but I knew if I did, he would find out and we would have a terrible trip back home.

The trip back home was very difficult anyway because I had several attacks. When we arrived home, I told him I thought I should go to the emergency room. He did not care and said, "You will be okay."

The next morning, he took the children to daycare and I took myself to the hospital. Not knowing then that it was my gallbladder, I explained the pain I had been in. I was taken into surgery right away. The next day, the doctor came in and told me it was my gallbladder, which was full of stones and very close to bursting. If I had not gotten medical help, it would have caused many more problems. The next week I was done, and he went back to live with his mother.

Chapter Four

With God in my life, I was attending church again. I had two precious children, and my life was filled with joy and love. I prayed each day, not just to ask Him for help, but also to thank Him for what He had done in my life. Not planning on ever getting married again, I continuously prayed for a better job and worked hard to get ahead for the three of us.

With God's help, I got a good job at a plant in Fort Lauderdale, building avionics equipment for commercial and military aircraft. I became interested in the purpose of the different components, which were diodes, capacitors, resisters, and transistors.

I was working on a VCO, which looked like a small rectangle metal box. Fitting the different components inside was difficult and I thought there must be an important purpose for each component. As a result of my curiosity, I went to school at night to learn circuitry and understanding schematics and design. Upon passing the course, I was promoted to the position of electronics technician. This doubled my weekly pay with better benefits, allowing me to purchase a new car and qualify for a duplex, which gave us rental income. The extra money made our lives better, as my ex-husband was not paying child support, which was absolutely fine with me.

If ye abide in me, and my words abide in you, ye shall ask what ye will, and it shall be done unto you. John 15:7

The job of an electrical engineer was to design different kinds of avionics equipment. The avionics were built for commercial airlines, as well as military aircraft. The assembly lines were organized by stations, each performing different tasks to assemble the units. At the end of the assembly line, we had to test the completed units.

As an electronics technician, my job was to make sure each unit was properly tested and passed all specifications before being passed on to shipping. If there were problems with the specs, it either went back to engineering or the specs manual had to be rewritten. When problems were found, we worked alongside the engineers that designed the piece.

I thank my Lord for being with me through the hard times. I often felt alone, but never lost faith. If I had not been raised in church, learning to love and trust in Him, my life would have been very different.

I went through many difficult times—being a shy unhappy young child that wanted to see my parents happy, not wanting to see my siblings in trouble or my father upset, and being a wife that took on all I could do, even when it never seemed to be enough. Many times, I just wanted to hear my parents say they loved me. I was very insecure and spent a lot of time alone, so I thank my mom and grandmother for always talking to me about God.

Train up a child in the way he should go: and when he is old, he will not depart from it. Proverbs 22:6

One day, my children and I were at the beach building sandcastles. I remember the feeling as if it were yesterday. I had no one to share my two beautiful children with; no one to share how fun they were; no one to share the cute things they were doing every day.

When I got home, I called my mom and said, "Mom, I think I want to come back."

She said, "No, don't. There's nothing here for you and you are doing so well in Florida."

I was hurt, but she went on to say, "I love you and I knew I never had to worry about you. I always knew you would be okay. Remember, God is with you."

She then reminded me of these two verses:

"Yet I am always with you: you hold me by my right hand." Psalms 73:23

Until now you have asked nothing in HIS name. Ask, and you will receive, that your joy may be full. John 16:24

Chapter 5

One of the engineers working with me on these specifications was a very nice gentleman. We were able to quickly see where the problem was and sent the unit back to engineering.

Not working on that problem any further, I went on to other units. However, this gentleman would come by my station each day to say good morning. I never thought anything about it; I would just say, "Hi."

He was smart and handsome, much more than I had ever dreamed of. Plus, I believed that old saying; ***the good ones are always taken.*** I was sure he was most likely married; never even thinking he could possibly be interested in me.

On Friday nights, my ex-husband picked up the children from day care and had them until Saturday at 6 pm. Our company had a bowling league on Friday nights, which was fun, and I enjoyed that time out.

My ex-husband showed up at the bowling alley one night, after I had gone out to dinner with him the previous week. I had mistakenly felt hurt for him. He did not have our home anymore and he was only seeing the children one day a week. On top of that, he was living with his mother. I felt I should try to make him happy. After dinner, he had made the comment, "You can't do this on your own."

He was not paying child support, so he probably felt I needed him. By that time though, I had worked too hard to hear that.

So when he showed up at the bowling alley, he was hoping we would get back together, but I knew it would never work. I told him so and added that he would be in my prayers and I would always wish him the best. When I left the bowling alley that night, I found the driver's side window of my car smashed. He left a note stating if we were not going to get back together, then I should get a divorce.

The next day he called and asked again whether I wanted to get back together or get a divorce. I could care less about getting a divorce, because I could care less about ever getting married again. I told him if he wanted a divorce, he could go get one.

One night after work, a friend asked me to go on a double-blind date. I declined, but looking down the aisle I pointed and said, "I sure would be interested in him, but the good ones are always gone."

She responded, "Pat? He's not married."

I could not believe it. He was still coming by every morning to say good morning.

I was twenty-seven, and very happy picking my children up from daycare and going home. The couple that owned the daycare have been my friends now for 53 years. She was the teacher and her husband was the fire chief. To this day, she says she remembers when I would pick up the children and say, "Going home, fixing dinner, getting in bed with my two children, one in each arm, and falling asleep." This great couple became my close friends and we did a lot together. Not being married, I felt safest with them, a married couple, rather than with single friends.

On Sunday, January 12, 1969, my friend that owned the daycare and our children attended church. On the way home, her husband called to tell her he had two tickets on the fifty-yard line at the Orange Bowl. I knew nothing about football at that time, but we headed down I-95, meeting her husband at the gate. We got our tickets and found our seats. When we looked in front of us, we saw Johnny Carson! My friend's husband, being fire chief, was hired to chauffeur Mr. Hess, the owner of the New York Jets, and that is how we got such great seats.

This was Super Bowl III, in which the Baltimore Colts lost to the New York Jets, 7-16. Don Shula was coach for the Baltimore Colts at that time and Joe Namath was quarterback for the New York Jets.

The company I worked for transferred from Baltimore to Florida, due to the unions in Maryland. Many of our top officials and engineers were from Baltimore, Maryland.

I found out later that Pat was one of the engineers that came from Baltimore and had actually stayed at the same hotel the Baltimore Colts stayed during that time. Not knowing him at that time, I had placed New York Jets flags all around my station.

Monday was now going to be very interesting. I could not wait for him to walk up and say good morning again. I was disappointed though, because he did not come by that day.

Tuesday, after being at work for about an hour, I glanced up and saw him coming toward me. I was excited to see him and wondered if he would speak to me again. I had my head down and was doing my work, feeling him getting closer. Finally I heard him say, "Good morning."

I did not just say hi this time; I said, "Good morning! How are you?" I had a photo of my children on my desk. He commented about my great looking kids and asked how old they were. Just a little bit of small talk and he was gone again.

The next day, the engineer that taught my electronics class came by and asked how I was doing. He said he had been keeping an eye on me and since my promotion he had heard I was doing a great job. I thanked him for sharing that with me. He went on to say, "You know, there is an engineer upstairs that likes you."

I said, "Really? Who?"

"Pat."

He told me Pat wanted to ask me out, but that he wanted to get a new car first.

I said, "Really? Well, next week the company is closed down for two weeks and I will be on vacation."

Hourly employees always had two weeks off over the 4th of July. Salary employees still worked and scheduled their own vacations.

I had plans to leave early Saturday morning to drive to Fayetteville, North Carolina to visit my aunt and uncle, stationed at Fort Bragg Army base. My baby brother, then sixteen, flew down to Fort Lauderdale, where I picked him up before we headed north. We had a great time visiting, but my mind was on getting back to work. The two weeks came to an end, with my brother and I attended church with the children. After church, we got lunch and headed home.

Upon my return to work, I felt concerned that this great guy was way out of my league. I figured he most likely met someone else during my two weeks off. However, around 10:30 I looked up and he was headed my way. I was breathing so hard, but hoped he would not notice.

When he got to my desk, he says, "How was your vacation?"

I could not even process what he said, because I was thinking, *Wow! He is still interested.*

That day he asked me on a date for Friday night. I was on cloud nine all week. Friday night could not get here quick enough. He picked me up in his new Pontiac Grand Prix. We went to a movie and then for coffee; we talked for hours.

Next day on the way to work, I ran over a sharp object in the road and my tire was going flat. I was right around the corner from work when, miraculously, there he was coming down the road. He stopped and fixed my tire for me. He told me months later that he felt so good to be able to help me that day.

We continued dating for months. One Friday night, sitting on a bench on the beach at Lauderdale by the Sea, he asked me to marry him. I probably hurt his feelings, but I could not in good conscience say yes that night. I wanted him to meet my children, and for them to meet him.

I believe God places things in our path to listen to and use in the future. God is our conscience and we need to listen to that. This is one of those times that we should,

Hear counsel, and receive instruction, that thou mayest be wise in thy latter end. Proverbs 19:20

When I was age five, we all took a train to visit my grandmother. I was playing in the front yard with my cousins and ran into the house to go to the bathroom. At the top of the stairs was the bedroom my parents were staying in, and the bathroom was right next to their room.

I heard them, so I looked in and said, "What are you doing?"

They were under the covers and my daddy said, "It's okay. I'm just rubbing Mommy's back."

I said, "Okay," and went to the bathroom and ran back down stairs.

However, I never forgot that, and it played a big part in my life. Being single, I never allowed men I dated to come into my home. I never wanted my children to see anything at five, or any age, that they may look back on. I never wanted my children to see me with one man one day and later, another man. This was important to me.

I never brought Pat to my home, but now deciding to marry, I wanted my children to know him. A week later, I explained this to Pat. He understood and I accepted his proposal. I started inviting him over for dinners and we did fun things with the children.

Making your ear attentive to wisdom and inclining your heart to understanding. Proverbs 2:2

I also introduced Pat to my married friends, and we spent a lot of time together with them. My friends stood with us in marriage, and their two children decorated our car. We were married at the Methodist church in Fort Lauderdale.

Chapter Six

Many of our friends at work thought I would quit now that I was married. I did not quit work though; my two precious children were my responsibility. I always did my part to care for them. I did not want anyone to think I got married for Pat to take care of us. I married him because I loved him. I continued working, doing my part, because my children were and always would be my responsibility.

For our first Christmas together, Pat built a Christmas garden. I was not familiar with the concept, but it was big in Baltimore. It was a 4x8 sheet of plywood, he painted areas showing green grass and roads.

It had three sets of trains going up the hills and through the tunnels. He placed houses, cars, hotels, and a church. It was a complete little village, with an area in the middle to place the Christmas tree. It was beautiful! Robby was eight at the time and he loved it.

In 1971, Pat and I had our beautiful baby boy. We named him Michael. He weighed nine pounds and two ounces. I had never seen such a proud daddy. Michael made us a complete family. Before, I had worked hard for my two children, but now we both worked hard together for our three children.

On Thanksgiving Day, 1971, we fixed our complete dinner, which included turkey and all the trimmings. We wrapped everything tightly with foil, and headed north into the Ocala Forest. We set up camp, and sat down to give thanks, all holding hands, even baby Michael's little hand.

It was so beautiful in the forest, listening to the birds and watching the squirrels jumping from tree to tree. Robby loved butterflies, and caught them in his net before letting them fly away. It was a special time for us in the Ocala forest.

This may strike people differently, but when I pray, I always start by giving thanks to my Lord for all He has done in my life. A lot of people only go to our Lord in prayer when they have a need. We need to talk with Him each day, just giving thanks. He will always be there in our needs, but we should not just ask without giving thanks every day.

I will praise thee, O Lord, with my whole heart; I will tell of all thy marvelous deeds. Psalms 9:1

I will praise the Lord according to HIS righteousness, and will sing praise to the name of the Lord most high. Psalms 7:17

On December 13, 1972, our second son was born. At about 2:30 in the morning, we were headed to the hospital and Pat asked, "What about a name if we have another boy?"

I stated, "We won't have a boy. We are having a girl, and her name will be Michelle."

He responded, "But if it is a boy, what do you think of the name Christopher?"

Back in the seventies, we did not have ultrasound, so we never knew the sex before birth. About 9:30 in the morning, I woke up and Pat said, "We have a Christopher!"

When I saw him, he was so perfect, and I was so pleased to have another son.

I always say, God is good all the time and all the time God is good. HE gave us another great little boy.

Chapter Seven

During the summer of 1972, eight-year-old Sandi fell off her bike. I ran to her and saw her ankle was bleeding. Picking her up, we went into the house to get medicine and a bandage. It seemed like she walked with a limp way too long.

Having an appointment with Michael's pediatrician shortly after, we told him about Sandi's fall. He looked at her ankle and then watched her walk up and down the hall. He said he wanted a neurologist to look at her.

He made a phone call and the neurologist came down, being in the same medical building. His name was Doctor Crevlin. he again had Sandi walk up and down the hall as he watched. He told Pat and I he wanted to do further testing. We set up an appointment the next week.

It was difficult to watch what my little girl went through at that appointment. She had an electromyography (EMG) test, which measures the electrical signals in her muscles. This test delivered mild shocks in the nerves as the doctor recorded the responses.

These shocks were done up and down both legs and arms. Sandi cried out, "Mommy, have him stop!"

I laid my whole body across hers, holding her and crying myself, but not wanting her to see me. The test took about thirty minutes. When it was finally done, we had Sandi go into the playroom, while

Pat and I went into the doctor's office. He asked questions about our families, regarding any medical conditions. We told him that Sandi's biological father had muscular dystrophy. He stated muscular dystrophy was not hereditary, but he would still like to examine him. We gave the contact information to the office to set an appointment for her biological father to come in.

A couple weeks later, we got the call to come in and talk with the doctor regarding the results of the test. We were told my ex-husband had come in and that he did not have muscular dystrophy. The doctor explained that for many years all muscular problems were combined together under a dystrophy. Different doctors started sorting them out. CMT was named after these three doctors, Charcot-Marie-Tooth. Doctor Crevlin told us there was no treatment for CMT. We were told to keep Sandi active and moving in her daily chores and activities.

In thinking about messages I believe were from God, as a child, I thought my parents were not worried about me when I could not walk. However, my grandmother sat me down and told me they were concerned, they had not wanted me to worry or be concerned. We did not want Sandi to put her head down at night and worry, but I worried and cried when I saw her hurting.

In raising Sandi, we had her involved in everything the boys did. She never knew it, but we were very concerned, and I spent many nights in prayer. Often, Sandi came into our room and say, "Mommy, my legs hurt so bad."

I would get up and rub her legs with alcohol. Sandi was so special, and she had such a great personality; when she walked into a room it was like sunshine. I knew then how my parents felt, because I never wanted her to worry and break her beautiful spirit.

Our boys loved water skiing and Sandi loved it as well. She had a kneeboard and enjoyed being pulled behind our boat. She, like her brothers, was a great swimmer; they all loved the water.

When Sandi was in high school, she had many friends. She was class president of her senior year. We attended the Friday night football games and would see her friends grab her and carry her up the bleachers. We had a summer home on Lake Lure in North Carolina, and she would jump off the boathouse into the lake. We never held her back from things she did, wanting her to live as normal life as possible.

When she graduated from high school, she got a job. She applied for and received an American Express card, which was difficult for a young person to get at that time.

She was never aware of our concerns. She went to her job at five in the morning, when it was still very dark. The employees had to park far out in the parking lot, allowing customers to park closer to the store. We were always concerned that if someone grabbed her, she would not be able to run to get away.

At one of her appointments with Doctor Crevlin, he told Pat and I that whatever we were doing to keep it up, because she had a beautiful personality. She never let things bother her. One day, she came home from school and said a boy called her handicapped. She said, "I told him he was too, because he wore glasses." That was her attitude; she was very secure within herself.

My brother, Dean, died of an aneurysm, and while I was in New York with my family, Sandi called and told me Warren asked her to marry him. She had been dating him for a long time, and Pat and I loved him. However, the time now was right in front of us that we needed to talk to her about CMT and it being inherited.

I prayed about this, asking my Lord how to handle it. It was a very hard conversation, but she had to know the details. After explaining it all to her as easily and thoughtfully as I could, I felt I lost part of my daughter that day.

In 1986 at the age of twenty-two, Sandi married Warren. It was a beautiful wedding, and we had a brand new home built for them in Wellington, Florida.

They had two beautiful daughters, born in 1992 and 2001. God was so good! Sandi is a Christian and raised her beautiful family in church. I know she has had many difficulties over the years with CMT, however, still to this day she has the same spirit and personality she always had.

We had always been very close, but a lot changed after that. However, even with that, I would not have changed a thing. She has always been independent and is living a bright and joyful life. We wanted her life to be filled with meaning and purpose. Physical and mental well-being includes taking care of your mind with positive thinking and expectations. We always said, no one would ever take advantage of Sandi.

> *Get wisdom, get understanding: forget it not; neither decline from the words of my mouth. Forsake her not, and she shall preserve thee; love her, and she shall keep thee.* Proverb 4:5-6

Chapter 8

After Sandi was detected with CMT around her ninth birthday, we had a home built on Lake Eden in Delray Beach. This allowed her to have a lot of exercise while swimming every day. After moving to Lake Eden, I wanted to spend as much time as I could with the children. I continued working as an electronic technician until I took my Florida Real Estate Test and got my license.

I loved selling real estate, and it allowed me the freedom to be with my children, especially during the summer months when the two older ones were out of school. We spent many days enjoying the beach, as well as boating on the weekends.

We had a neighbor that would always say she could not wait for school to start so her kids would go back to school. I loved the time I spent with my kids though; summers with them were so enjoyable and very memorable.

Four years later, I went back to school at night and got my business license and my real estate broker's license, and opened my own real estate franchise.

Chapter 9

Pat's job as an electrical engineer constituted applying physics and mathematics in designing avionics equipment and systems for the airlines, military aircraft, and Air Force One. So many times when we were out to dinner, he would grab a napkin and start drawing circuitry to explain a design that was in his thoughts. He often traveled on different airlines, such as Delta, to show a design that could help them.

Radar was one of those units that were placed on Air Force One. Pat had security clearance and flew on Air Force One, visiting the Pentagon several times. He told the children about Air Force One only being called Air Force One when the president was on it. If the vice- president was on it, it was called Air Force Two.

He also flew on planes with Air Force colonels, sometimes for days, getting refueled in the air. One time, he had been flying for several days, longer than expected and needed clothes. He contacted me from the Lockheed C-5 military aircraft and had me bring clothes to Patrick Air Force Base, located in Brevard County, Florida.

When Mike, age fourteen, and Chris, age twelve, and I got there, we saw a huge military airplane, and the boys both said, "Mom, that must be it!"

Only a few minutes went by before we saw a much larger aircraft fly over us. It was the Lockheed C-5, which made the first plane, a Lockheed C-141, look small.

The engines could not be shut down, so a gentleman from the plane brought Pat's suitcase out and I gave him the one I had brought. The boys and I stayed and watched the huge C-5 take off again. What an amazing experience it was for the boys and me to see.

Chapter 10

In 1986, when Sandi got married, we built them a new home at the same time we were building ours. We owned two airplanes, a Cessna 172 and a Cessna 152. We built our new home in a development called Wellington AeroClub. This was a community like no other.

We moved into our new home November 1986. Having our airplanes right in our back yard was so nice, because now Pat was flying back and forth to work. Several different times a year, we got together with other neighbors, sometimes three or four airplanes flying together over to the Bahamas, or up to River Ranch in central Florida for lunch.

The newspaper wanted to do an article about Pat flying to work, so the journalist writing the article went on a flight with Pat and our son, Chris. When she wrote the article in the paper, she entitled it, *JUST PLANE FOLKS.*

PLANE FOLKS

A plane in every driveway? At Florida's airdrome communities, it's more than a flight of fancy.

Chris, at the age of fourteen, started flying with Pat. A friend of Pat's from work was a flight instructor, and we paid him to fly with Chris so all the hours would be properly logged. We also paid for Chris' flight school in order for him to formally take the tests.

To get his FAA private pilot's license, he had to log thirty-five hours of flight time. He had to also pass the written tests and pass the FAA check ride. He accomplished everything, and on December 17, 1989 at the age of seventeen, he received his private pilot's license.

Chris had always loved airplanes and as his parents we saw his potential. After high school, we sent him on to the Aviation Academy to get his A & P licenses. The FAA issues the certificates for airframe and power plant, and this qualified him as an aircraft mechanic.

Michael always had many friends. At fifteen, he started working at a new hospital, painting walls. When he turned sixteen, I remember taking him to get his driver's license, and right from there he wanted to go apply for a job at Publix Supermarket. He was so proud as he walked out smiling; he got the job.

Michael worked himself up into management and then retired, later becoming a bank manager. Years later, he went back to college and got his degree in Information Technology.

In 2020, we had many unspoken prayers going out for Michael.

Chapter Eleven

With Pat having heart problems, it grounded him from flying. His job was all about aviation though, so he still got to fly with others during the designing of new avionics equipment. At times, he would fly for days, the plane getting fueled in the air.

After open-heart surgery in 1992, Pat decided to retire after thirty-three years on the job. However, a major company in Atlanta, Georgia, called Pat and asked him if he would consider joining them, giving them at least one year. Pat loved his job, and this was a company he had worked with for years, designing avionics for them. After much consideration, he did retire from the company in Fort Lauderdale and joined the company in Atlanta, Georgia.

In August 1992, the company paid to move our family from our home in Florida to Atlanta. The day of our move, Hurricane Andrew was predicted to hit the Palm Beach area, but at the last moment went further south and instead hit Homestead. The company took over the sale of our home in Florida, and sold it within sixty days.

We purchased a home in Woodstock, Georgia, which was not flat like south Florida. It was beautiful; our home had a 500-foot winding, hilly driveway through the woods. We had a lake close by, where we had a boat slip.

After arriving in Georgia, Mike stayed with our pets while Pat, Chris, and I drove back to Boca Raton, Florida where our airplanes where kept in hangers. Chris flew the Cessna 152 and Pat flew the

Cessna 172 back from Boca Raton, Florida to Ball Ground Airport in Canton, Georgia.

Can any mother imagine what that drive back to Georgia alone was like for me, knowing my nineteen-year-old son was flying that distance alone? He had been flying for a couple of years, but never that distance.

One very hot day, after moving to Georgia, Pat was on his way home from work. A family of deer was heading to the water, but the fawn laid down on the hot blacktop and stayed there. Pat stopped the car and picked him up before driving up our driveway.

I could not believe it when I saw him carrying a fawn in. He brought him into the kitchen, and we put a cold cloth on him. We hurried because we were concerned about him being separated from his parents. When we took him back down to the end of our driveway, his parents were just feet from us, waiting. When we put him down, they all ran off together. Several days later, they were in our back yard, close to our back patio. You could see they were not afraid of us at all.

During the time we were in Georgia, our two boys married. Sandi had two beautiful daughters, making us very proud grandparents.

One year turned into nine years before Pat retired for the second time.

Following are Pat's five retirement letters from family and friends (8/27/2002).

As we get older, I look back at the many dreams I had, the many challenges that went along with those dreams, and the many successes I had along the way.

Dreams, as a kid, was wanting to always do what was right, to get the love and affection from my parents. THEY NEVER SAID THEY LOVED ME. But now I would love to have the chance to tell them both that I love them and I understand now how hard it must have been to raise five children.

As I got older and became a mom, it was the happiest time of my life. I remember holding Robby and Sandi. As I would look at them, I knew no one in this whole world could possibly be happier than me. Robby and Sandi were my life—my whole entire reason for being.

I let my babies know how much I loved them. I told them every morning and I told them every night. It was a big challenge for me, raising two children on my own. I had many dreams for the three of us and worked very hard toward reaching those dreams. I went back to school at night and continued my education. I got a promotion at Bendix into the test department. As an electronics technician, I owned my own three bedroom two bath pool home in Plantation, FL. At the age of 26, I purchased a duplex and had both sides rented with a very good income, as well as my job at Bendix. I always drove a new car and I had my two children in a private school.

Those were the years that I was able to work hard. I was proud and felt good about myself, because of the things I accomplished for the three of us. I had good morals and set very high standards for myself. I never let myself down. Don and Esther Piers were my two closest friends. We always did things together as a family. That made me feel safer with my two babies. I was not looking to get married again. I was very happy working hard at accomplishing my own goals. But when I met you, it was not long before you became my best friend. You had a great reputation and very high standards. I knew I was falling in love. When you asked me to marry you, I was very proud and honored to become your wife.

You have never let me down. At age 29, you became Daddy to my two babies—and at age 31, we had two beautiful sons. We then had the challenge of supporting, protecting, loving, and educating four children—all under the age of 10. The dreams I had for my two children, now became our dreams for our four children.

You never set in one place—you always worked hard and continued educating yourself, so as to make things continuously better for all of us. You gave us all a very good life. We had new homes, new boats, new campers, new cars, motorcycles, ATCs, go-carts, airplanes, and on and on. Our family had more and did more than most families could ever dream of. Our life was our children and we enjoyed having fun with them. You had a great career, but you made it what it was. It was not just handed to you.

Our dreams for our children were to give them a standard of life that they would want to continue for themselves. We wanted to start our children out on a path in life, that each of them would set dreams for themselves—that they would work hard to meet the many challenges that would appear and the many successes to enjoy along the way. But we always hoped they would not forget the ones that supported them and helped get them there. As parents we only wanted to be loved, respected, and remembered—knowing that we can be happy and enjoy the few years we have left.

We both felt this retirement would never come. We felt we supported our children far too many years, without thinking financially about us in our later years. But if we had to do it all over again, we would not change a thing. I would like to say to you today, that you have given me a wonderful life and you have allowed my dreams, our dreams, and our children's dreams to come true in so many ways. When they say your golden years, I never realized just what they meant. But these past few months, waking up with you each morning and going to bed with you each night mean more to me than I could ever say. With your efforts in working these last few years, we have been able to get ourselves very comfortable financially.

Now we have the Golden Years in front of us. You are my husband, my lover, and my best friend. I want to thank you for choosing me to go down this road of life with you.

From your wife, your lover, and your best friend.

Dad,

I want to express how much you mean to me. You are my best friend, father, and brother. I felt like I lost all three when you moved away. It has affected me in a way that I'm only now realizing. We had such great times together, better than most friends or fathers and sons have. I want to continue having those good times with my dad.

I'm so proud to have you as my father. There's not a time that goes by when I'm at work that I don't think about you. I sometimes don't say enough to you about how proud I am. I tell people I work with how my dad was one of the key engineers in developing the weather radar on the B-767. Every time I walk in front of an aircraft, I stop and daydream— thinking back to those times that you were on business trips, helping companies like Delta with radar problems.

You have always been there for me and I have taken that for granted. Your hard work supported a family of four, while having a demanding career. I can't begin to realize how tough that was, but I feel like I have gained so much from your hard work. I have learned a great deal about responsibility and dependability because of you. Let me explain.

Responsibility: You supported a family of four. You always gave and never asked for anything in return. Never once did I hear you complain about things that may have happened at work.

Dependability: I felt very secure in my family, because I knew if I needed my dad, he would be there. You had a 43-year career without skipping a beat. You never questioned Mom on anything she ever spent on us *kids. I'm only hoping I can do the same for my family, like you have done for us. You prioritized your time with the family, while most fathers would have chosen drinking with friends and chasing women. I feel like that is the reason I'm the father and husband I am today, because I grew up in an environment where you put us first and everything else was second and third.*

I gained so much from your aviation career. These were the building blocks for my career. I enjoyed and will always cherish the times we have together with our own airplanes. I still talk about what we used to do to them. I still remember me in the garage at 14 years old, riveting the doubler plate on the wheel pants and putting the nose cowl on. Now look where I am—standing next to a B-767 that I just finished a sheet metal job on. I'm writing this from work, where I think of you so much and where my mind is the clearest, sometimes.

I want to continue this relationship as father, best friend, and brother with you—and now add grandfather to our little boy, yours and mine.

Love always,

Your son,

Chris

RESPONSIBILITY

Responsibility means many things to many people. To me, responsibility means being there when you are needed, holding yourself accountable for your own actions, making sacrifices for the ones you love and setting examples through everything that you do. I am not aware of what it is like to have the responsibilities of a father, but you have given me an example to strive for. One part of that example I would like to touch on is your responsibility as an earner, breadwinner, or contributor.

Sometimes I wonder, what makes me get up every day and go to work? Seems like a simple question, but I think not. There is more to this that just the easy answer of needing money, paying bills, or it's what I am supposed to do. I believe that it has more to do with the morals and values instilled in me from the time I was a child and old enough to understand. You went to work every day, every week, every year. It is easy as a child to be selfish and self-serving by thinking that their father isn't home enough. We have all thought that during our childhood. But, now as an adult, I understand what it means to be a responsible person. I understand what it is like to go to work every day (even when you don't feel good) and earn a living. I understand the enjoyment of being self-sufficient. I understand sacrifice, selflessness, and above all else, responsibility.

I believe that a person learns more through example than through being told. That is what you have given me, Dad, an example. You have worked hard through the tough times, through the good times, and all of the in-between times. You have raised a family through your hard work, diligence, and fortitude. You have made our life more comfortable and enjoyable. You have done everything that a father can do to help ensure the success of his family. You have given each of us the chance to be the best we can be—and for that I am thankful. You have made your contribution to the workforce and your family. Now, it is time for you to take the next step in life—that step being retirement.

Retirement sometimes sounds like an end. I think it is a beginning. It is the beginning of the rest of your life. Retirement is the culmination of all of the things you have accomplished earlier in your life.

You are a good father, husband, and son. I am proud to call you my father—not only because of who you are, but because of who I am, because of you.

In closing, I would like to once again thank you for everything you have taught me, given me, instilled in me, and been to me.

Love,

Michael

————————————

Dear Daddy,

I want you to know that you are so deserving of retirement. I am so happy for you to be able to have your dreams come true. I know you have always wanted to live on a lake again. You have had all you have ever wanted and it is because of all your hard work over all these years. I really don't understand a lot about your career. I know that you were in the Air Force. I know that you had a lot to do with the Pentagon. I know that you have flown on Air Force One. I know that you know Air Force Generals. I know that you are very respected by commanders and generals in the Air Force. I remember you would have to go on business trips and get in front of a lot of people to speak about some new product that you and your company designed, to get them to buy it. Which would get your company multi-million dollar contracts.

When my friends would ask, "What does your Dad do?" I would say that my dad designs radar that is in airplanes. I know that that is just the surface of your career, but that in and of itself is very impressive!!

I can't really go on and on about all the incredible things you have done for your government or your company. That was your first career. Being a dad was your second career. That I can go on a little more about.

(You aren't allowed to retire from your second career.)

The thing I know the best about you is how wonderful a dad and granddad you are. Some of my earliest memories are of you helping me learn to ride a bike and building a pool for us. I also remember when I cut my head on your table saw—you wrapped bandages around my head and put a feather in it to make me look like an Indian. It took my mind off all the blood coming down my head.

When we would go to Lake Ida and go boating for the day, you would make scrambled eggs with cheese and bacon. Then when we moved to the lake, the weekends were spent boating and pulling me on the knee board or some other things we would try. We would go camping the weeks that you were on vacation from work.

I remember when I would need something done to my bike, you would fix it. Then you would give me some silly receipt for fixing it. I remember you letting me drive your Datsun 200SX. I remember the beautiful wedding Mom and you gave to Warren and me and helping us with our first new home.

I remember having to be careful not to compare Warren to you, when we first got married. As the years have gone on, he feels more comfortable coming to you to ask your opinion about things. I still come to you and Mom for your opinion on things.

I thank you for always being there for us over the years. Thank you for being a dad to Warren and helping him learn the qualities of being a good dad and husband. I know he has learned a lot from you and your dedication to your family. Thank you for being a wonderful granddaddy to our girls. The special things you do with and for them, I know they will always remember and cherish their times with you—just like I do.

Thank you for your dedication to your career. We all benefited in a lot of ways. We had just about anything we wanted. We learned a lot about responsibility, good work ethics, how to strive be to the best we can, how important family is—just to name a few. The thing I have learned the most is that you love your family more than words can say. I as so thankful that I have had the opportunity to share my feelings with you. I am so proud to be able to call you my DAD!!

Thank you for everything.

I love you!

————————————

Dear Patrick (Pat)

Well, today is the day when I feel inspired to write to you, to congratulate you on your retirement.

What a wonderful word—retire. As a child, to retire meant you were old and had nothing else to look forward to.

But now that we are there, too—in some ways it is the best times of our lives—to be able to do what we want, when we want.

You, at an early age, had the foresight to see how electronics and aviation would be the cutting edges of technology—many advances effect our everyday life every single day—and apply it in such a way that you not only a valuable engineer to Bendix, but were eagerly approached to join the Lockheed staff. So you have not only retired once, but twice. What an accomplishment!!!

The best part of all was how patiently and carefully you were able to give to your children—especially the boys—some of your knowledge and ability. So that now they—Chris and Mike—have responsible jobs and are far more advanced in their abilities to deal with people; repair cars, boats, planes, jets, etc., etc., etc. than most people; and best of all, how to be a good husband and father. All within a setting that most children dream about, but will never experience—not even as adults.

With your job you were able to travel the world, meet people, and be involved with the upper echelon of the military and governments. Your being involved with some of the equipment put on Air Force One was not only an honor, but an indication of what your abilities are, and what you are capable of—and how you were entrusted with the very best of people, but also the equipment.

We are proud of you and your accomplishments and especially happy about your 1. Retirement ---and your 2. Retirement.

It has been a long time coming, and yet when you look back over the years, you probably wonder—as we do—how we got here sooo quickly---and still feel sooo young, well in most ways.

Sorry, Pat! Now for the biggest job of all:

· Teaching your grandchildren
· Answering all of their wonderful questions Like:
    1. Why is the sky blue?
    2. What makes grass green, etc, etc, etc.
    3. How do black cows give white milk, and so on.

So that one day they can be heard saying—

  May Grandpa taught me about:

- *All the wonderful places he traveled*
- *Fishing*
- *Skiing*
- *Playing ball*
- *His story, etc. etc.*

The best is yet to come—

  Since this is Thanksgiving week, we want you to know how thankful we are that you are our friend---and without Sally, as our friend first, we would never have met you— God is good!

  You are blessed with wonderful children and beautiful grandchildren, and a wonderful wife. A blessed man!!

  Enjoy your retirement—enjoy every day.

  Have a wonderful Thanksgiving!

                    With love,

                    Don & Esther

All the different times he'd spent on flights, he always remembered flying over Lake Hartwell, a beautiful lake in South Carolina. We started looking for a house in Anderson, South Carolina.

How fitting with Pat's heart problems, that we now moved to his dream location on Lake Hartwell. During that move, we got a call that Robby had died. I went to my Bible that night and read:

And ye now therefore have sorrow: but I will see you again, and your heart shall rejoice, and your joy no man taketh from you. John 16:22

I will not leave you comfortless; I will come to you. John 14:18

Chapter Twelve

My oldest son, Robby, was always a sweet little boy. He had such a great personality, always doing things to make people laugh.

At the age of fourteen, he would make commercials with his younger brothers. He had them each sit in lawn chairs by the lake, with an umbrella, and Coca-Cola cans in their hands. As they drank, he videoed them, and then made the little recording into a Coke commercial. He would also throw a Frisbee into the air and take a photo, making it look like a UFO.

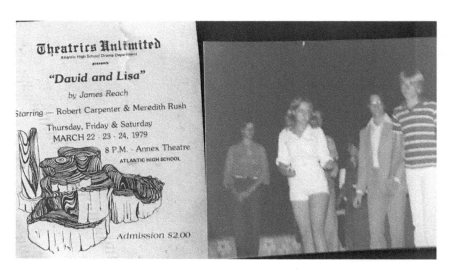

My Mom always made a lot over Robby and he loved making her laugh.

When he was in high school, he was in drama and was very good. After high school, he worked at Publix Supermarket, but still acted at the community playhouse. At twenty-one, he left home and went to Hollywood, California. He felt he could become an actor, and I believe he would have been great at it. However, things did not go that way for him. Robby was born September 7, 1962 in Hollywood, Florida, and died in Hollywood, California on December 19, 2001, at the age of thirty-nine.

This was the first time I actually knew, and could feel, how my Mom must have *felt*. She lost her son (my brother) Dean from an aneurysm when he was forty-four. We all grieved when he died, never realizing then how much harder it had to be for her.

Robby loved butterflies. I remember when he was only four or five years old, we were driving down the road when Robby saw a butterfly and said, "Mommy, look it's a monarch!"

I did not even know what a monarch was at that time. I did not understand why I thought about that while I was grieving, but that day I mentioned it to Pat.

Our son, Chris, worked for Delta Airlines at that time, and they helped by flying Robby's body back to us in South Carolina. I stayed up all night, crying my eyes out and typing words to Rob.

Letter to Robbie on December 19, 2001:

ROB, I'M SO SORRY

You are home now, Rob—home with Mom and Dad.

When you were small and as sweet as could BE,

The world was so PERFECT, as I could see.

When we put you to bed and turned off the light,

We knew you were safe all through the night.

The hugs, the kisses, and the "I love you's"

Were things that were easy for us TWO.

We would sit and talk, sometimes all night long,

Never EVER thinking things could go wrong.

As you grew older and started drifting away,

We could only hope you would return one day.

Months and days turned into years

And, as your parents, we shed many a tear.

But when you called us with pain in your voice,

It was time for healing once and for all.

You said, "I love you" and you wanted to come home.

We started the process in getting you here.

We had our long talks once again

And said the things each wanted to hear.

You talked about the Christmas' we had,

And how nice it would be, to be there this year.

Rob, I'm so sorry, I didn't know.

But tonight is Christmas Eve and you are with us (Mom, Dad, Sandi, Warren, Chelsea, Holly, Michael, Chris, and Tiffany). Your family once again. This Christmas is for you, Rob.

We will start the service at about noon, standing and viewing only you. We will touch you and kiss you once again, and say our last goodbyes. Then Dad, Michael, Chris, and Warren will carry you to a beautiful car, where we will all go for a very short ride.

Once we get to your resting place, you will be placed next to where Mom and Dad will be. You won't be alone again. On your stone it will read, "The Final Resting Place for Robert Scott."

Rob, I am so sorry. We all love you and we want you to rest in peace.

Goodbye for now, Rob. Dad and I love you so and we will forever be by your side.

MOM

Before Delta brought his body back to us, we went shopping and I bought a bracelet that had this verse on it:

Today shall thou be with me in paradise.
Luke 23:43

We placed it on his hand.

I also bought a tee shirt with a butterfly on it for him to wear under his white shirt, thinking he might be cold. Weird—I know!

But now he is dead, wherefore should I fast? Can I bring him back again? I shall go to him, but he shall not return to me.
2 Samuel 12:23

Chapter Thirteen

Our home in Anderson, South Carolina, was a large home on a beautiful lake—three bedrooms, three bathrooms on three acres, all enclosed with a three-rail white fence. This was where we spent our golden years together from the end of 2001 until September 2009.

Many nights, we fixed our dinner on the pontoon boat and set out on the lake, waiting till the sun went down. We saw so many beautiful sunsets.

We attended the Baptist church and made many good friends.

We went to bed each night, arm in arm, saying our prayers together and waking up each morning, giving thanks to GOD for waking us up. We had such peace.

Pat had feeders for the squirrels. I loved the hummingbirds, and always had feeders for them. Our life was good and so peaceful.

Three times a week, we went to the nursing home to read devotional books to the residents. We enjoyed them, and they looked forward to us coming. We were allowed to bring our little shih tzu, Mindi, and the residents loved her.

Wake up, and strengthen the things that remain, which were about to die; for I have not found your deeds completed in the sight of my God. Revelation 3:2

Waking up each morning, we had coffee on the patio overlooking the lake. In the early mornings with the lake looking like glass, we would get on our two Waverunners and ride down to the dam. It was such a large lake; we could ride for thirty-five miles in any direction at forty miles per hour. So early in the morning, the lake was calm, and we would see deer come down to the waters edge, and hear the birds singing so beautifully. It was certainly a piece of God's country.

Early morning on September 17th, sitting on our patio drinking our coffee, a beautiful butterfly landed on my shoulder. Pat immediately said, "There's Rob."

I said, "Oh wow!"

It was a feeling I could not describe, and I stopped breathing for a few seconds. I stayed very still for the longest time.

The next morning, my soulmate, Pat, was gone. At 6:30 am on September 18, 2009, my soulmate, partner, and best friend went home to be with Jesus.

I called 911, and sat waiting in the rocking chair on the front porch, overlooking our beautiful green lawn enclosed in the white fence. Thinking about how much Pat and I loved cutting the lawn, or sitting in our golf cart, looking over our home with a cold drink in hand. Suddenly, a butterfly hovered and landed on my right hand. I could not move, watching the butterfly and thinking about the one the day before. I hoped it was the same butterfly. It has never happened again since then.

It was difficult getting through those very early days. However, the butterfly experience never left my mind. One day, I decided to see what the Bible said about butterflies. I found there were ninety-three Bible verses related to butterflies. This is one:

Therefore, if any man be in Christ, he is a new creature: old things are passed away; behold, all things are become new.
2 Corinthians 5:17

Chapter Fourteen

Selling our home in South Carolina was very difficult; it was the home where we spent our golden years together. Losing my best friend and soulmate was harder than anyone could ever know. My children were hurting in their own way after losing their dad. However, my life was turned upside down and inside out, everything had changed. He was the only person I ever absolutely loved, and the only person I ever felt genuinely loved me. He made me feel special with just a look.

Our relationship was about doing for each other without expecting anything in return. I felt so loved when he expressed joy and happiness just seeing me happy, which was opposite of my experience in any other part of my life.

Love becomes empathy for the other person's emotional state, which I felt I always had for my siblings, my parents, my ex-husband. However, until this great man came into my life I never felt that come in my direction. It grew over thirty-nine years; we could finish each other's thoughts and sentences. He said he loved to see me laughing and happy. He gave me credit for accomplishing so much in my life; thanking me for being a great wife and mother; grateful for how I handled our family finances.

God brought this man into my life. Every step throughout my life brought me closer to him; my life as a child; marrying my first husband and moving to Florida; going back to school at night for two years; and being promoted to a electronics' technician, which allowed me to meet him in the first place. God gave us our two great sons, and gave me a life I could have never imagined when I wrote down on paper at my mother's kitchen table the things I thought I wanted.

I will meet Saint Peter at the gates of heaven, and waiting just beyond those gates, I KNOW I WILL SEE MY SOULMATE COMING TOWARD ME ONCE AGAIN. We will be together throughout eternity.

Then shall the dust return to the earth as it was: and the spirit shall return unto God who gave it. Ecclesiastes 12:7

For by grace are ye saved through faith; and that not of yourselves: it is the gift of God — Ephesians 2:8

My sister stayed with me for quite a while, helping to settle things after Pat's death. My two sons and daughter were all living in different parts of the country and I would have been by myself in South Carolina. I decided I could not live by myself in that big house, so I started looking for a new home. I needed to spend time with my siblings, so I went to Watertown, New York, my old hometown.

I found a beautiful modular home, buying it in 2010, and making it my primary home in 2016. For those years after my spouse died, I rented the home in South Carolina on weekends. It was a very desirable three-bedroom, three-bathroom house, with a hot tub and a game room with pool table and other games. We were very close to Clemson University, and people came from all over for the college games on the weekends, as well as the many fishing tournaments taking place on the lake.

Chapter Fifteen

In 2017, Reggie, my oldest brother died. My sister lived in the same house for sixty years with all her children living around her. I felt I had to get back to where my life was for many years. I had a cousin, a brother, and close friends living in Florida.

In 2019, I decided to move back to Florida. It was where I met my best friend of thirty-nine years, and where we raised our family. Florida held so many memories for me.

In November 2019, I purchased a beautiful home in a 55+ gated golf club community in Florida. Arriving in November, I had only been there a short time before COVID-19 hit us in 2020.

It was a tough time because everything closed. I was so thankful God lead me back from New York just before COVID-19 hit us. Everyone had to wear a mask, and staying six feet apart was suddenly called *social distancing*. People could not work because everything was closed and everyone had to stay inside their homes.

After COVID-19 hit in February 2020 and not being able to leave my new home, it gave me plenty of time to write my book.

This is how God lead me:

I closed on my new home in Florida on October 29, 2019, while still being in New York. On the 30th, I placed my home in New York on the market and drove out of New York on November 1st. I arrived in Florida at my new home on November 3, 2019. By November 8th, 2019, I had a contract on my home in New York, which closed right after Thanksgiving.

I will instruct thee and teach thee in the way which thou shalt go: I will guide thee with mine eyes. Psalms 32:8

For thou wilt light my candle: the Lord my God will enlighten my darkness. Psalms 18:28

No tears. God gave me a great life, allowing me to experience many things. Many times I was in the valley and many times I was on the mountain, having faith it was all for a reason. God was with me all the way and He was always the same.

I thank my Lord every single day.

I have fought a good fight, I have finished my course, I have kept the faith: 2 Timothy 4:7

To every thing there is a season, and a time to every purpose under the heaven. Ecclesiastes 3:1

Remember ye not the former things, neither consider the things of old. Isaiah 43:18

Conclusion

To finish this book, I want to state where my children are today:

Michael works in Information Technology (IT). He is married to Kristy, who is a registered nurse (RN). They have the sweetest little boy.

Christopher works in the field of Aerospace. He is married to Tiffany, who works for BlueCross Insurance. They have two of the greatest children.

Sandi is married to Warren, who is an electrician. They have two beautiful daughters.

I have five grandchildren. The oldest, at this time, is twenty-seven, and the youngest is seven.

Our children were raised with a mom and dad that always told them we loved them. We gave them a great life and taught them good morals. They were taught they could do anything they set their minds to. We taught them the importance of integrity by guiding them to be honest and have strong moral principles, as well as to stay true to themselves.

Loving each one of my children, I still have many things yet to enjoy and look forward to, like seeing and enjoying my great grandchildren, yet we don't know what life will be tomorrow.

I hope and pray every day that each of my children and my grandchildren will know HIM

Behold, the Lord's hand is not shortened, that it cannot save; neither HIS ear heavy, that it cannot hear Isaiah 59:1

And we know that all things work together for good to them that love GOD, to them who are called according to HIS purpose. Romans 8:28

Acknowledgments:

First and foremost: My LORD who has been in my life for 78 years.

Second: My husband, GP (Pat), born April 4th, 1941, and died September 18, 2009. I am thankful he chose me to walk down life's path with him.

Third: My first son, Robby, born September 7th, 1962, and died December 18, 2001. He made us laugh, we also had many tears.

Fourth: My three children, Sandi, Michael, and Christopher. They each played such an important part of my life, and each one of them was a precious gift from God.

Fifth: "Patrica Ann" My sister and best friend, thanking her for being there for me.

Sixth: My two special grandchildren, Camden and Corah, thanking them for always taking the time to make me feel important in their life, with just a quick text saying "Love you Grandma and miss you."

And Jesus answering saith unto them, Have faith in God. Mark 11:22

The LORD thy God in the midst of thee is mighty; he will save, he will rejoice over thee with joy; he will rest in his love, he will joy over thee with singing. Zephaniah 3:17

CPSIA information can be obtained
at www.ICGtesting.com
Printed in the USA
LVHW011755021120
670476LV00005B/303